Let's Get Mapping!

How to Read a Map

Melanie Waldron

Raintree

C333661453

Raintree is an imprint of Capstone Global Library Limited, a company incorporated in England and Wales having its registered office at 7 Pilgrim Street, London, EC4V 6LB – Registered company number: 6695582

To contact Raintree please phone 0845 6044371, fax + 44 (0) 1865 312263, or email myorders@ raintreepublishers.co.uk. Customers from outside the UK please telephone +44 1865 312262.

Text © Capstone Global Library Limited 2013
First published in hardback in 2013
First published in paperback in 2014
The moral rights of the proprietor have been asserted.

All rights reserved. No part of this publication may be reproduced in any form or by any means (including photocopying or storing it in any medium by electronic means and whether or not transiently or incidentally to some other use of this publication) without the written permission of the copyright owner, except in accordance with the provisions of the Copyright, Designs and Patents Act 1988 or under the terms of a licence issued by the Copyright Licensing Agency, Saffron House, 6–10 Kirby Street, London EC1N 8TS (www.cla.co.uk). Applications for the copyright owner's written permission should be addressed to the publisher.

Edited by Nancy Dickmann and Abby Colich
Designed by Victoria Allen
Original illustrations © 2013
Illustrated by HL Studios
Picture research by Ruth Blair
Originated by Capstone Global Library Limited
Printed and bound in China by CTPS

ISBN 978 1 406 24918 7 (hardback)
16 15 14 13 12
10 9 8 7 6 5 4 3 2 1

ISBN 978 1 406 24925 5 (paperback)
17 16 15 14 13
10 9 8 7 6 5 4 3 2 1

British Library Cataloguing in Publication Data
Waldron, Melanie.
How to read a map. -- (Let's get mapping!)
912'.014-dc23
A full catalogue record for this book is available from the British Library.

Acknowledgements

We would like to thank the following for permission to reproduce photographs: Alamy: pp. 7 (© avatra images), 9 (© The Art Gallery Collection), 11 (© Rob Walls), 13 (© Jim Wileman), 17 (© Dominic Byrne), 21 (© Radius Images); Corbis: pp. 23 (© Ocean), 27 (© Ashley Jouhar/ cultura); © Lovell Johns Ltd 2012: pp. 16, 28; Shutterstock: pp. 4 (© zhu difeng), 5 (© Anton Gvozdikov), 12 (© Mark Yuill), 24 (© Peteri), 26 (© Stocksnapper).

Cover photograph of boy reading a city map at a resort reproduced with permission from Superstock (© Corbis).

Background and design features reproduced with permission from Shutterstock.

Every effort has been made to contact copyright holders of material reproduced in this book. Any omissions will be rectified in subsequent printings if notice is given to the publisher.

All the internet addresses (URLs) given in this book were valid at the time of going to press. However, due to the dynamic nature of the internet, some addresses may have changed, or sites may have changed or ceased to exist since publication. While the author and publisher regret any inconvenience this may cause readers, no responsibility for any such changes can be accepted by either the author or the publisher.

Contents

Some words appear in the text in bold, **like this**. You can find out what they mean by looking in the glossary.

Marvellous maps

Most maps are flat drawings of the land. They show the land from a "bird's eye view". This means that they show what it looks like from above. Maps are full of information. They can tell you things about Earth's **natural features**. They can also tell you about the things that humans have built on the land, such as roads and buildings. Maps can even give you information about things that you can't see. For example, a map can show how much money people earn in different countries.

Maps can show a bird's eye view of roads like these.

What are maps for?

People use maps to help them travel around. We can also use them to find places, and to learn about places and the people living there. Maps can also be used to show how the land has changed over time.

People use maps to help them find their way around.

OLD MAPS, NEW MAPS

People have been making maps for hundreds of years. Many older maps were made by explorers using sketches of the areas they explored. Today, most maps are made with the help of **satellite images** and **aerial photographs**.

A world of maps

Different types of maps can show very different things about the same area of land. A map of your country might show the towns and cities, and the **borders** between regions. A different map might show how the land is used – for example, for farming or forestry. Some maps can give very detailed information about the buildings in an area.

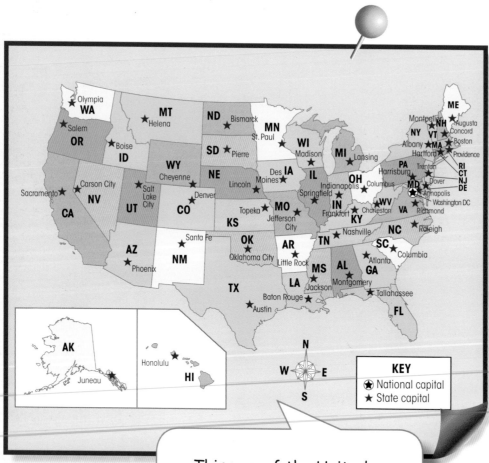

This map of the United States shows the borders between the states, and the capital cities in each state. State names are abbreviated.

Travel maps

Many maps are designed to help people travel from place to place. Road maps show all the roads in an area, and the towns and cities they connect. Railway maps show different railway lines, and the stations that link them together. Some maps show air travel routes across the world.

Maps of town centres are often displayed on notice boards. They can help people find their way around the town.

PAPER OR DIGITAL?

Many maps are printed onto folded sheets of paper, or bound into books. Lots of **digital maps** can be found on the internet. Some digital maps can be downloaded from a computer onto handsets you can carry around, like mobile phones.

Layers of information

There is a lot of information about the land that a map could show. It could show buildings and what they are used for. It could show the type of **vegetation** growing on the land. A map could show the many different streams, rivers, and lakes of an area.

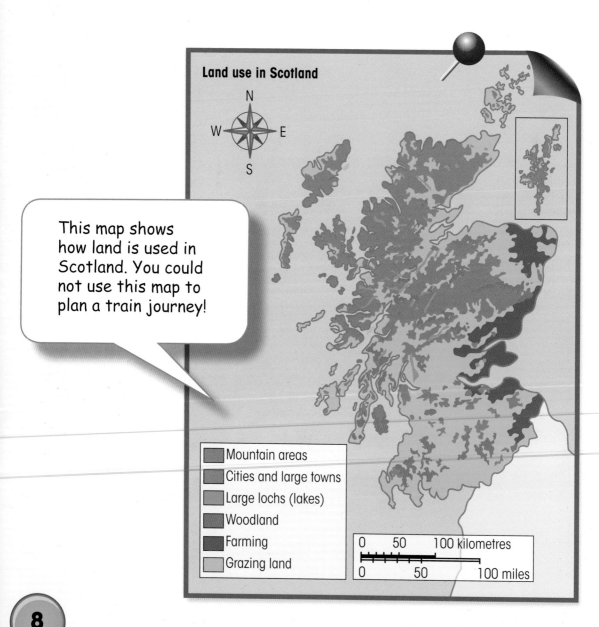

Land use in Scotland

This map shows how land is used in Scotland. You could not use this map to plan a train journey!

Mountain areas
Cities and large towns
Large lochs (lakes)
Woodland
Farming
Grazing land

0   50   100 kilometres
0   50   100 miles

Cartographers are people who make maps. They must select the information they need for each type of map they are making. To make a map of a town, showing all the different buildings, they would not need to show the type of rock underneath the ground.

Map titles

When you look at a map, it is important to understand what the map is trying to show you. The map title is a good clue! Make sure you read the title first.

UNMAPPED LANDS

In the 1700s, many European explorers travelled west across North America. They created and used maps as they went. Many of these maps had huge blank areas. These areas showed places that had not yet been explored.

Map symbols

Maps use symbols to represent different things. A symbol is a small dot, picture, line, or shape that is easy to spot. For example, a blue line might mean a motorway, while a black line might mean a railway line. Trees could represent an area of forest, and grey shapes could represent buildings.

If a map has a few different symbols, it should also have a **key** to explain what each symbol means. A key lists each symbol and what it represents. If a map has symbols, you should look for the key to help you understand the map.

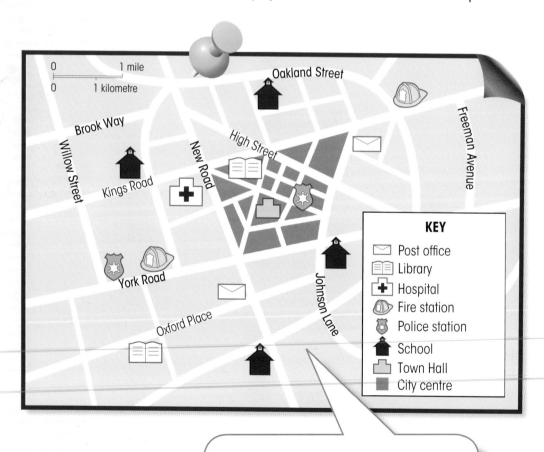

This map uses little pictures as symbols. Look at the key. Can you see why these pictures have been chosen?

PICTORIAL MAPS

It's not just symbols that can represent things on maps. Sometimes mapmakers draw tiny pictures of the actual buildings. These maps are called **pictorial maps**. They are mostly used in tourist towns. They are pretty to look at and they help people to find buildings or special places of interest in a town.

Which way up?

If you are using a map to help you find your way around, or to find a certain place, you need to make sure the map is the right way round! To help you do this, mapmakers usually print a **compass rose** on the map. This tells you which way is North, South, East, and West on the map.

N stands for North, S for South, E for East, and W for West. Some maps simply have an arrow with an N, to show which way is North.

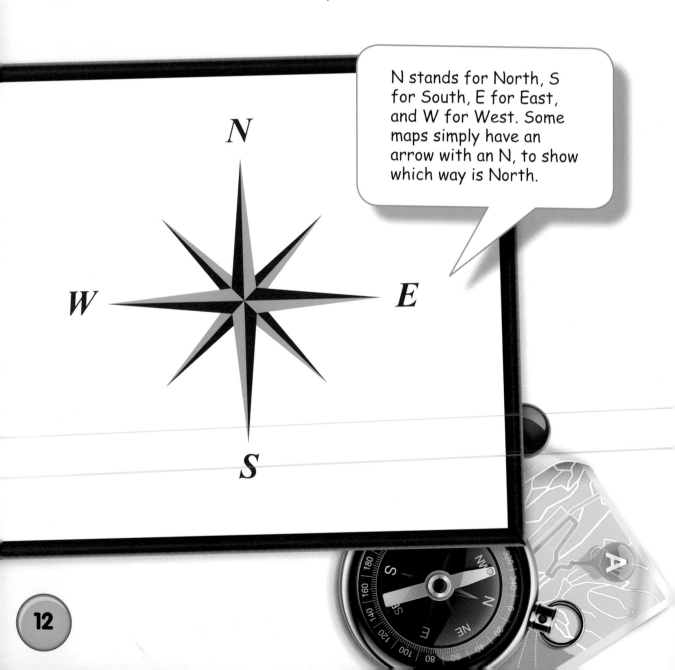

Finding north

The compass rose shows you where north is on the map. To make sure the map is the correct way round, you need to find where north is on the ground. To do this, you can use a **compass**.

The red arrow on a compass always points to North. Hold the compass flat and see which direction the red arrow is pointing towards. This is North. Now you can turn the map so that North on the map is the same as North on the ground.

Using a compass and a map together is useful in the countryside where there are no street names to help you.

Shades of colour

Sometimes maps are used to show different amounts or measurements of things. This could be the height of land above sea level, or the number of people living in an area.

Mapmakers can use colour to show how the amount of something changes across the land. For example, maps showing land height often show low land as green. As the land gets higher, the colour changes to yellow, then orange, then brown or purple. Very high land in mountainous areas is often shown as white.

This map shows the height of the land in southern Africa. Look at the key to see where the highest land is.

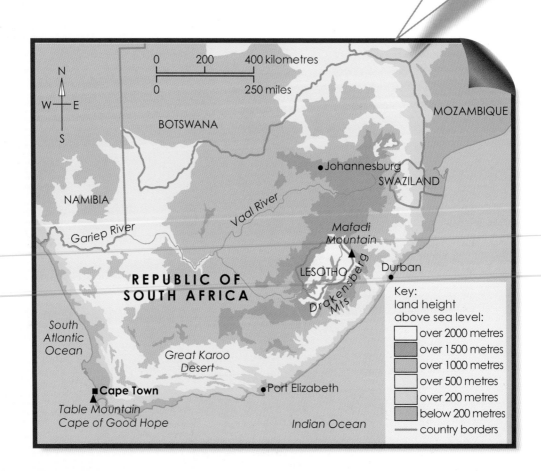

Similar shades

When you look at a colour-shaded map, make sure you read the key first. Then you will know what each colour represents. Sometimes, mapmakers use shades of one colour that are very similar. It can be hard to tell which colour is which on the map! But using shades can help you pick out patterns on a map.

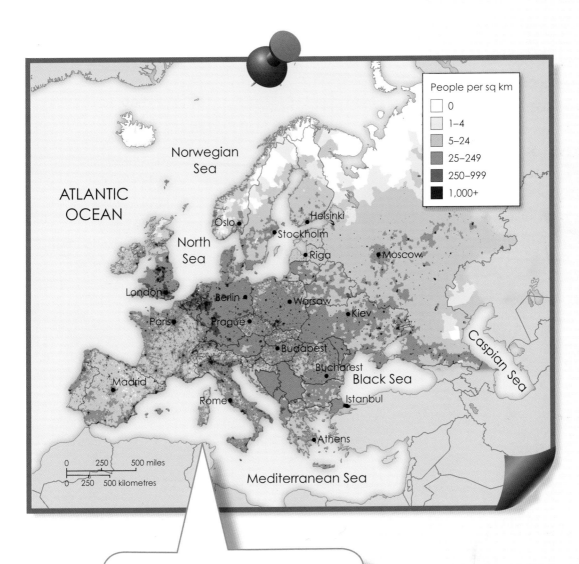

People per sq km
0
1–4
5–24
25–249
250–999
1,000+

This map shows where people live in Europe. You can see that there are lots of people living around the large cities.

Contour lines

Some maps give a lot of detailed information about the height of the land. These maps are usually of small areas, rather than whole countries or **continents**. People such as hill walkers and rock climbers use them.

Mapmakers use **contour lines** on maps to show the height of the land. Contour lines follow the land at the same height above sea level. For example, a 500-metre contour line would run along all the land that is 500 metres above sea level.

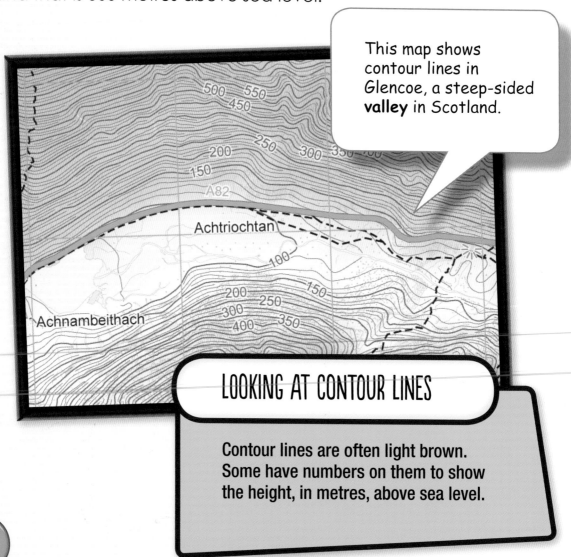

This map shows contour lines in Glencoe, a steep-sided **valley** in Scotland.

LOOKING AT CONTOUR LINES

Contour lines are often light brown. Some have numbers on them to show the height, in metres, above sea level.

Line spacing

Contour lines are spaced at intervals. For example, one line might show land that is 10 metres higher than the next line. Steep land is shown by contour lines packed closely together. This is because the land height rises by 10 metres in a short distance. Land that is quite flat has contour lines spaced far apart because there is a further distance to go before the land height rises by 10 metres.

You can see the steep valley sides in Glencoe here.

Map scales

Maps are always smaller than the land they show – otherwise they would be life-size! Maps are scaled-down versions of the land. This means that everything is shrunk down. Maps can be shrunk down by different amounts.

Small and large scale

Small-scale maps shrink everything down a lot. This means that a large area, like a whole country, can be shown on one map. However, there is not very much local detail on small-scale maps. Large-scale maps shrink everything down a bit less. This means that only a smaller area, such as a town, can be shown on one map. More local detail can be included on large-scale maps.

Scale ratios

Some maps have **scale ratios** written on them. A small-scale map ratio could be written 1: 250,000. This means that 1 centimetre on the map equals 250,000 centimetres (or 2.5 kilometres) in real life. This might be useful for going on a car journey. A large-scale map ratio could be written 1:10,000, where 1 centimetre on the map equals 10,000 centimetres (100 metres) in real life. This might be useful for finding your way round a town on foot.

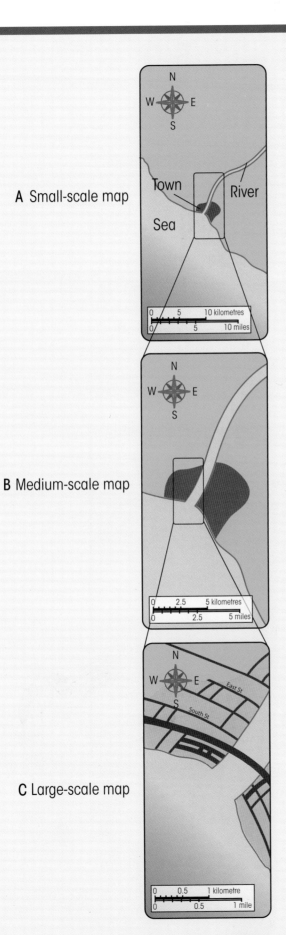

A Small-scale map

B Medium-scale map

C Large-scale map

These three maps show how the level of detail increases as the scale gets larger.

Finding the distance

When you are using a map, it is sometimes useful to work out a distance in real life. Many maps have a **scale bar** printed on them, to help you do this. A scale bar is a line, or a bar, that has distances marked on it. You can use a ruler to measure the distance you want to find out on the map. You can then hold the ruler against the scale bar to see how far this is in real life.

> Use the scale bar in this map to work out the distance between the park and the school.

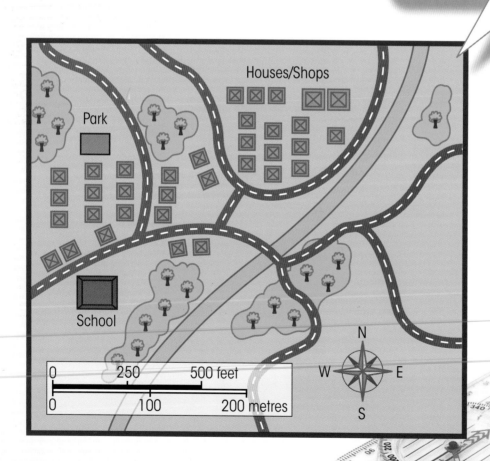

Measuring bendy lines

You can use a straight edge, such as a ruler, to measure distances between two points on a map. However, you might want to know the length of a river. Not many rivers flow in perfectly straight lines! You could use a piece of string to follow the river on the map, bending it around corners. You could then hold the string straight against the scale bar, to find out the distance.

It is useful to know how far a path might take you. You can use the scale to work this distance out.

Lines of latitude and longitude

Lines of **latitude** are imaginary lines that circle around Earth. We measure lines of latitude in degrees. The **equator** is a line of latitude. It circles all the way around the middle of Earth, and has a position of 0 degrees. Each line above and below the equator goes up one degree until the North and South Poles. They are 90 degrees North and South of the equator.

Longitude

Lines of **longitude** run from the top to the bottom of Earth. Each one passes through the North and South Poles. The **Prime Meridian** is the central line of longitude and has a position of 0 degrees. All the other lines are measured in degrees East or West of the Prime Meridian.

ORANGES AND CAKES

Lines of longitude all meet at the North and South Poles. They split Earth into wedges, like an orange. Lines of latitude never meet. They split Earth up into layers, like a round cake.

Lines of latitude run in parallel, straight lines around Earth. Lines of longitude are imaginary lines that run from top to bottom of Earth.

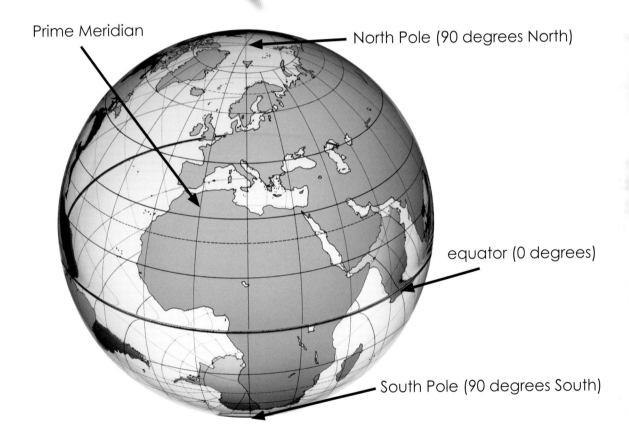

Prime Meridian

North Pole (90 degrees North)

equator (0 degrees)

South Pole (90 degrees South)

Pinpointing positions

We can use lines of latitude and longitude to find a location on Earth's surface. For example, the city of Moscow in Russia is where latitude line 55 degrees North meets longitude line 37 degrees East.

On maps of much smaller areas, lines of latitude and longitude are a bit too far apart to be useful. Instead, maps can use grids to help locate things. Grids are made up of lines running across and lines running up and down. They make small squares on the map. Often, the bottom sides of the squares are named with letters. The left side are named with numbers.

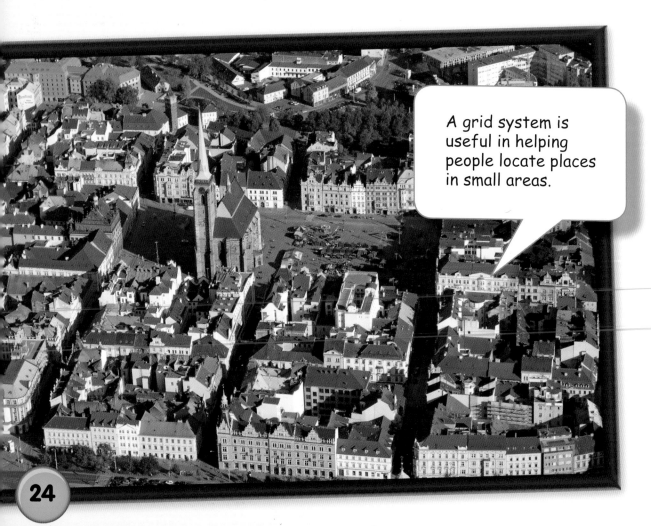

A grid system is useful in helping people locate places in small areas.

Using grid lines

All the squares on a map grid have their own **grid reference**. To find a square's grid reference, look at the letters running along the bottom of the map. Find the letter for the square. Now do the same for the numbers running up the side of the map. Put the letter and the number together, and you have a grid reference.

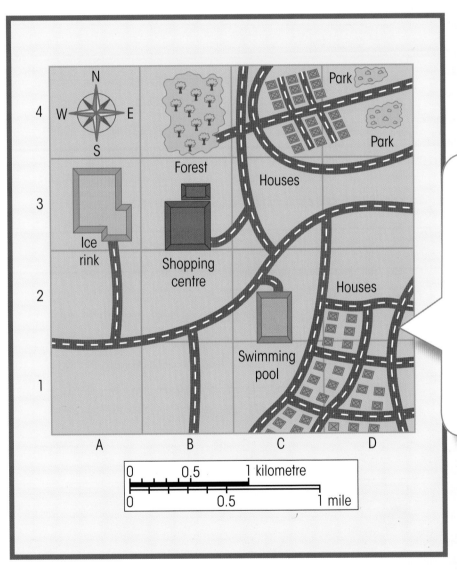

In this map, the square containing the swimming pool has a grid reference of C2. Can you find the correct grid reference for the square containing the ice rink?

Using maps

Map reading is a really useful skill! It can help you get around and find places. But with modern technology, you don't always need to be able to read a map. Satellites can send signals to receivers such as **GPS** handsets and even mobile phones. These can then show you on a screen where you are on the map. They can also direct you to where you need to go.

However, you should not always rely on this technology – batteries can run out and gadgets can break down. Learning good map-reading skills is important too.

GPS handsets can help you get around easily.

Remember some important steps in map reading:

- Make sure you have the correct map of the correct area.
- Make sure you know what the map is trying to show you.
- Make sure you know which way round the map should go – use the compass rose.
- Look at the map symbols and the key so you know what features to look out for.
- Look at the scale so you can judge how far away things are.
- Look at the grid to see if that can help you find the information you need.

Get mapping!

Look at this map. Can you use the title, key, scale, and grid to answer the following questions?

Town of Cheshunt, its transport links, and the River Lee Country Park

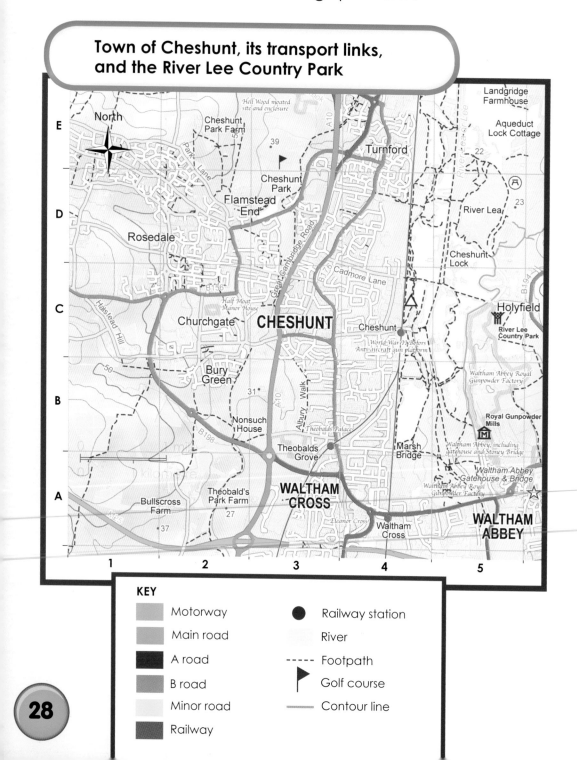

KEY

Motorway	● Railway station
Main road	River
A road	---- Footpath
B road	▶ Golf course
Minor road	—— Contour line
Railway	

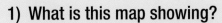

1) What is this map showing?

2) What is the green line running down the left side?

3) What is the pink circle in grid square C4?

4) In which grid square is Cheshunt Park Farm?

5) Is Rosedale north or south of Churchgate?

6) Find the contour line with a number on it. How high above sea level is this area?

7) What is the name of the river?

8) Use the scale bar to work out how far apart Waltham Cross train station and the golf course are.

ANSWERS

1) This map is showing the town of Cheshunt, its transport links, and the River Lee Country Park.

2) The green line is a main road.

3) The pink circle is a train station.

4) Cheshunt Park Farm is in grid square E2.

5) Rosedale is north of Churchgate.

6) The area is 50 meters above sea level.

7) The river is the River Lee or Lea.

8) Waltham Cross train station and the golf course are about 6.5 km apart.

Glossary

aerial photograph photograph taken from high above Earth's surface, usually from an aeroplane

border imaginary line that separates different countries, or different regions inside a country

cartographer person who makes maps

compass instrument with a needle that always points North

compass rose drawing with four points, showing where North, South, East, and West are on a map

continent one of Earth's seven major areas of land: North America, South America, Europe, Africa, Asia, Australasia, and Antarctica

contour line line that follows all the land at a certain height above sea level

digital map map that is shown on a screen, such as a computer or mobile phone screen

equator imaginary circle around Earth that is halfway between the North and South Poles

GPS (global positioning system) system that uses signals from satellites to find your exact location and direct you to another location

grid reference figure made up of numbers and letters, or just numbers, that allows you to pinpoint a place on a map

key list of symbols and an explanation of what each one represents

latitude distance between the equator and a point North or South on Earth's surface. The distance is measured in degrees.

longitude distance on Earth's surface that is East or West of the Prime Meridian. The distance is measured in degrees.

natural feature something on Earth's surface that has been created by nature, for example a mountain

pictorial map map with tiny drawings of the features it wants to show; often used in popular tourist places

Prime Meridian imaginary line on Earth's surface that goes from the North Pole to the South Pole and passes through Greenwich in the UK

satellite image picture, like a photograph, that a satellite can take of Earth from space

scale bar bar or line on a map which shows us how far a distance in real life is represented on the map

scale ratio number that tells us how far a distance in real life is represented on a map

valley long area of low land between two steep, sloping hillsides

vegetation all the plants growing on Earth's surface

Find out more

There is a whole world of maps and mapping waiting to be discovered! Try looking at some other books and some websites to start you off.

Books

Reading Maps (All Over the Map), Kate Torpie (Crabtree Publishing, 2008)

Using Maps (Maps and Mapping Skills), Meg and Jack Gillett (Wayland, 2011)

Using Maps (Ways Into Geography), Jillian Powell (Franklin Watts, 2012)

Websites

www.bbc.co.uk/schools/barnabybear/games/map.shtml
There is a game all about matching map symbols to their meanings on this website.

www.bbc.co.uk/scotland/education/sysm/landscapes/ highlands_islands/mapskills/index_intro.shtml#focus
This interactive site helps you to learn about compass skills, grid references, symbols, keys, and scales.

mapzone.ordnancesurvey.co.uk/mapzone/index.html
This is an interactive site all about maps and mapping, with homework help, maps, photos, and games. The teaching resources section includes lots of useful sheets about map skills.

www.oxfam.org.uk/education/resources/mapping_our_world/ mapping_our_world/l/home/index.htm
On this site, you can do puzzles and games, and see some different kinds of maps.

Index